# Table Of Contents

## Contents

<u>How to Measure ROI Metrics With Google Analytics</u>

# The Three Biggest Myths of Social Media ROI (And The Real Truth Behind Them)

Before we get started with the 5-Step Plan for social media ROI, I thought it would be useful to highlight some of the biggest myths about social media marketing return on investment, which are also some of the major reasons why brands either don't bother with it, or do not manage to benefit from it as much as they could be. Perhaps these myths (and the truth behind them) will help dispel some of your own beliefs, and aid in 'cleansing' your mind as you get ready to start anew!

**Myth #1: Measuring 'Likes' and 'Followers' = Social Media ROI**

**The Mistake**

Vast swathes of marketers calculate social media return on investment based simply on the number of likes or followers that their profiles on Facebook, Twitter, Pinterest, and others amass over a set period of time.

**The Truth**

Instead of 'likes' and 'follows', businesses need to focus more on traditional, overarching business marketing goals, which social media can also help them achieve. These include increasing sales, improving customer service, or expanding their customer base.

**Myth #2: Measuring Social Media ROI is the Same As Traditional Mediums Like TV and Print**

**The Mistake**

Marketers are so used to spotting and measuring the direct impact of social media on their audience, that they fail to spot how social media marketing differs.

**The Truth**

Unlike traditional marketing methods such as TV, radio, or print advertising where the impact of an ad might only influence one person on a single occasion, return on investment via social media must take into account the effects of amplification. When someone is interacts with social media content by liking, commenting or sharing, there is a good chance that someone else will be notified of this and check the content out too.

## Myth #3: Social Media Should Be Measured Independently Of Other Channels

### The Mistake

Thinking that is too difficult or impossible to measure social media marketing in a mix with traditional means of marketing such as TV, print, or radio.

### The Truth

Measurement of return on investment by traditional and new (social media marketing) means must be integrated in order to appreciate the full, combined effects of your marketing efforts. Dozens of free and easy-to-use social media analytics and reporting tools make this job more manageable than ever.

# Social Media ROI Plan Step 1: Define Business Objectives And Social Media Goals

When a business undertakes a traditional marketing drive in print, TV, radio etc., there will always be specific strategies and expected outcomes planned and detailed before the wheels are set into motion. Depending on the business type, the goals will be different, but typical examples include a desire for the business to:

- Increase brand awareness
- Drive leads into the pipeline
- Drive traffic to website
- Reduce customer service cost
- Improve customer satisfaction
- Improve customer retention and loyalty
- Increase sales

Social media marketing should aim to achieve the *same overall business objectives* as traditional marketing, but the goals of social media marketing and the metrics needed to evaluate the success of a campaign to align this with your *overall business goals* differ. There are a myriad of social media metrics, and the type used differs between the sorts of businesses who use social media marketing too. Typical social media goals include:

- Determine what customers and prospects are saying about your company via social media monitoring
- Gather competitive intelligence
- Engage with customers and prospects online
- Build thought leadership through sharing relevant content
- Maximize reach of content and messaging in social channels
- Support existing sales and marketing campaigns
- Support recruiting and retention efforts

- Build a customer community to provide support and advocacy

As you can see, social media goals are dissimilar to cold, hard business metrics. You should humanize your approach and factor this into ROI by measuring outcomes such as exposure, dialogue, interactions, support, advocacy, etc.

When you have an idea of the kind of goals you can achieve with social media, you must next decide **what you are going to do with it and how these goals will benefit your business as a whole**. For example, ask yourself:

- What could you do with direct, continuous customer feedback via social media channels?
- How would customers helping other customers help build your brand image?
- If you could use social media to reach more of your target audience, how would that benefit your business?

If you ask any business or marketer what they want to achieve with social media, their goals will be to *"get more customers and make more money,"* but as you now know, you need to figure out your *specific marketing and communication goals for social media* before you can start to make this happen for your business as a whole.

# Social Media ROI Plan Step 2: Identify Your Audience: Who Do You Want To Reach?

Once you have planned out what business objectives and social media goals you are trying to achieve, the next step is to identify which social networks will work best in helping you reach your target audience. One of the biggest mistakes many brands make is to sign up to every social network going, post the same content on each furiously for a week or two, only to give up when their fan count hasn't hit 50,000 and their conversion rate is zero. Therefore, it is essential to know who you are trying to reach so that you invest your time and money in the right channels.

As a crude example, Pinterest is the third biggest social network in North America behind Facebook and Twitter, so it's an essential tool for all businesses to utilize... right? Not necessarily! At present, Pinterest's user base is comprised overwhelmingly by females, and some of the site's most popular content is fashion, DIY, and crafts. If you are the owner of a beefcake men's boxing club, perhaps it isn't the best place to focus a lot your initial time and energy.

Facebook is a given for most brands due to its dominance in the field, but as a secondary or tertiary string to your bow, sites like LinkedIn and Instagram might work better for brands that are business-to-business-focused or rely on visual marketing respectively.

Develop a detailed picture of your target audience and take some time to research which social media platforms will work best for you and your business. If your target audience is wide-ranging, it might help to segment them by demographics, identify their needs, and develop behavior-based profiles based on these needs. With this information, you can work on creating content that will resonate most with each target audience.

# Social Media ROI Plan Step 3: Creating Content For Social Media: The Biggest Mistake Businesses Make (And How to Avoid It)

Steps 1 and 2 of this plan will allow you to plan out what you're trying to achieve and who you're trying to reach. Step 3 is where you can begin to think about what type of content will support your social media goals and resonate with your target audience. If you're looking to produce effective social media marketing content, there is one piece of advice that, if followed, will put you MILES ahead of the majority of companies on social media at present, and it's this:

**People, on the whole, do not use social media sites to be sold to.**

Too many brands focus way too much on their overall business objectives, spamming their followers with sales-orientated, self-promotional content that at best turns fans away from engaging with your material, and at worst gives them the impression that you are a company that doesn't care about anything but profits. As we will touch on further in the next chapter, social media marketing works best when it is made personable and conversational, not like the Facebook version of QVC!

With this in mind, you don't want to swing too far in the other direction either. If your social media updates are exciting and engaging, but do not align to help drive you towards your goals (and eventually, your overall business objectives), then you'll be wasting your time again. As much as social media is about being personable and keeping hard selling to a minimum, you should always keep your overarching business objectives in mind.

**The key to social media marketing that helps you see a healthy return on investment is balance.**

As I write in my bestselling Kindle book, *500 Social Media Marketing Tips,* an easy way to balance out your social media output is to think of the rule of thirds - share your own stuff a third of the time, stuff related-in-topic but from another source a third of the time, and interact with your customers and help them out on a one-to-one basis a third of the time. This should help you maintain a healthy balance between keeping your customers engaged and moving towards your goals and objectives.

# Social Media ROI Plan Step 4: Killer Techniques For Powerful, Engaging, Social Media Content

You may be asking yourself what exactly is the type of content best suited for social media? That very much depends on your target audience and the social networks that you have figured out will likely work out best for you. However, there are several general techniques that will work on whichever social networks you choose to focus on. Here are few simple, powerful strategies to get you started:

**Be Human And Sociable**

By its very nature, social media involves direct communication between individuals. It's this type of interaction that people most identify with on these kinds of sites between their friends and family, so be sure to mimic this with your brand. Of course, your tone of voice might differ between, say, Facebook and LinkedIn, which have completely different audiences and purposes, but either way a consistent tone of voice that makes brands sound like humans and not faceless machines of Capitalism is essential. For clear examples of what I mean, check out the social profiles of any major brand - Coca-Cola and Starbucks are great examples.

**Use Images And Videos**

Social sharing of images and videos is *huge*, and the way that social media is consumed by audiences mean, in many instances (Twitter being the most obvious exception in some respects), these more easily-digestible snippets of content often work better than text alone.

**Keep Updates Short**

This one relates again to the way that social media is consumed. When people are at home or on the go, they will *skim* through their news feeds, so if your updates are a wall of 1,000 words time and again, chances are they will be ignored. Tweets are a good standard to limit yourself to - 140 character chunks of texts.

**Be Consistent**

A company's social media presence that appears abandoned is the digital equivalent of turning your lights off. Because you're not updating online, people will assume that you're going out of business, even if the opposite is true. In reality, the opposite is true. Even if you are extremely busy, make time to update your social media sites consistently. This is doubly important if you communicate directly (to solve customer service issues and the like) via social media. Don't leave them hanging!

**Re-Purpose Content**

It is worth emphasizing that something that might be distributed as one piece of content in the real world (a press release, say), can be marketed as four or five content pieces for social media - blog about it, tweet, make a video, share on Facebook, etc. This is a fantastic strategy, particularly if you do not have tons of hours to plough into your social media marketing.

**Slow and Steady Wins The Race**

Social media success does not happen overnight, and that is always worth remembering. Just like in real life, friendships and bonds between you and customers can take a long time to build. Keep plowing away to see results. As mentioned above, I have seen so many instances of businesses leaping into social media marketing with gusto, only to give up shortly afterwards because they did not have 1.3 million Facebook fans and a ton of sales after their first week. Be patient!

This is only a tiny fraction of general advice for giving your social media marketing the best chance possible, but each social network has a myriad of techniques specific to them to help boost your efforts - way, *way* too many to go into detail here. If you're interested in learning hundreds of essential tricks of the trade for sites including Facebook, Twitter, Pinterest, Google + and more, do check out my bestselling Amazon Kindle book, *500 Social Media Marketing Tips.* Search for it in the Kindle store, or click the following links:

**Amazon.com:** www.amazon.com/Social-Media-Marketing-Tips-ebook/dp/B007L50HE6

**Amazon.co.uk:** www.amazon.co.uk/Social-Media-Marketing-Tips-ebook/dp/B007L50HE6

# Social Media ROI Plan Step 5: Measure and Adjust: Think Awareness, Engagement, Action

Once your social media marketing campaign is up and running, it is essential to keep track of your progress as you go. After all, if you don't know how impactful (or not) your efforts are, you will not be able to tweak or adjust them accordingly or accurately measure your return on investment. Measuring social media ROI can be challenging because of the sheer amount of information you *can* attempt to measure, but the key is to focus on the metrics that will help you best understand if you are hitting the social media goals you set in Step 1.

Before we look in detail about how to measure different metrics on the most popular social networks in a few chapter's time, it is a good idea to think about organizing the people you attract with social media (your target audience) into a traditional sales funnel (or just a 'funnel' if sales aren't part of your objectives) to measure them on their journey with you. It goes a little like this: lots of people will fall into the top of the funnel as fresh leads (i.e. everyone you attract to your social network profiles), and it is your job to keep as many of them engaged and on side as they filter down and out the narrow end, where hopefully they will be converted out as people aligned with your social media goals and overall business objectives, whether that be to drive them to sign up to your newsletter, create brand advocates, visit your website, buy your product, etc.

To make it a little easier for you to visualize, imagine splitting the social media funnel into three sections: **Awareness, Engagement, and Action.**

**Awareness**: These are the people at the beginning of your social media funnel. Through whatever other marketing, whether offline or on (business cards, Google Ads, e-mail signatures, product packaging, etc.), they have been made aware of your social media presence and have visited one of your social media profiles.

**Engagement:** Once someone is aware of you on social media, the next objective should be to move them down the funnel into a state of Engagement. An engaged fan will not only read your content, but positively participates with your content, whether that be through sharing, liking, commenting, or clicking through to links that you post.

**Action:** In many cases, ultimately you will want your engaged social media followers to take action, in what will be the final push in helping to reach your social media goals. As mentioned, this could be all manner of things depending on your specific objectives, including converting them into making a purchase or having them use your social media channels for customer service issues.

When you segment your social media measuring up into the three areas of **Awareness, Engagement, and Action,** it not only makes the task of tracking your metrics less daunting, but also allows you to more easily see where along the process you are performing well, and where things might be faltering and due for change.

For example, let's say you are a clothes store owner who wants more people to purchase products through your website. After analyzing your social media marketing following a couple of months, you notice that you are making lots of people aware of your social media presence, *and* they are engaged by clicking across from your social networks to your site, but not really converting many of them into sales. This would suggest a problem in the **Action** part of the funnel, which could be a poorly designed website, unappealing stock, or that you are promoting the wrong type of product to your followers.

# Social Media ROI Plan Step 5a: Follow the SMART Method

SMART metrics are Specific, Manageable, Actionable, Relevant, Trending, which makes them ideal for creating a system to benchmark social media efforts. Let's break it down:

**Specific:** You and anyone else working on your social media campaigns should be clear about what your goals are - the goals should be well-defined and clear to anyone that has a basic knowledge of the project.

**Measurable:** The metrics you choose to see if you are reaching your goals should be quantifiable using the reporting tools available. The goal should have a finite end and you will know when it has been achieved.

**Achievable:** Your goals should be achievable, based upon the resources and capacity of the people carrying out your social media marketing.

**Realistic:** Your plan for social media marketing should aim to obtain the goals reflected in your business objectives in a realistic manner.

**Time bound:** Set yourself a time period in which you believe your social media goals will accomplished, after which you can take some time to evaluate your progress. Enough time will provide an achievable challenge, whereas too much can affect project performance.

When you next plan to run a social media marketing campaign, take a moment to consider whether your goals are SMART goals.

# Putting It All Together: The 5-Step Plan Conclusion And Re-Cap

I must clarify all of the information above by stating that the benefits of measuring social media ROI effectively will, in the vast majority of cases, not be seen over night. And when the results do start to form into something of a lucid picture, they might not be the ones you want to see! Poor engagement levels, terrible click-through rates, little to no conversions... these are all part of the marketing game sometimes. However, at least you will have hard evidence to show you what has gone wrong and, with the metrics that you have measured, a clear vision of *where* things aren't performing well. Then you can sit down again, plan future campaigns and experiment to see how things change with an altered approach.

By following this logical 5-Step process, you will be in a position to monitor and analyze the social media metrics that can be aligned with your overall business goals and measure it up against the investment - **in terms of both time and money**. And as I said, best of all, you'll be rid of the confusion and uncertainty of social media ROI and in a position to build and develop your marketing strategies with confidence.

To recap, here are the 5 Steps:

Step 1: Define Business Objectives And Social Media Goals

Step 2: Identify Your Audience: Who Do You Want To Reach?

Step 3: Plan Your Content Strategy - Don't Be Salesy, Be Human

Step 4: Create, Engaging, Social Media Content

Step 5: Measure and Adjust: Think Awareness, Engagement, and Action

Step 5A: Follow the SMART Method

The following chapters will provide you with information about numerous free social media tools for measuring and reporting on metrics using the SMART method detailed earlier on.

# FREE Tools to Measure and Report Social Media ROI

There are a whole myriad of tools and dashboards (both desktop and web-based) out there to help you measure and track your social media metrics and, ultimately, help you calculate your return on investment.

While there are plenty of paid options that promise to amalgamate data from lots of the most popular social media websites in one place - HootSuite, PageLever, CrowdBooster, TwentyFeet, Social Bakers, Zuum Social, and more (and I would certainly recommend taking a look at them if your scope and budget is big enough), in the next few chapters we'll explore some of the most popular analytics tools that are free to use but nonetheless provide clear, useful data for social media ROI.

Pooling together the data from several analytical tools might be a little bit more of an effort (especially as the majority do not allow you to export data offline to programs like Microsoft Office Excel), and you may not get some of the *super* detailed information you'd get if you choose a paid option. However, as you'll find out, tools like Facebook Insights and sites like bit.ly, amongst others, are more than capable of providing you with useful measures that you can study to help build and adjust your social media marketing strategy.

One last tip or two before we get down to the nitty gritty: If you are unfamiliar with the following tools, I would recommend spending some time to understand at least their basic workings before you embark on a social media marketing campaign for which you want to measure ROI. Not only will this ensure that the metrics you measure are as accurate as they can be (avoiding problems with continuity further down the line), but building a meaningful report that you can analyze periodically will also become much, much easier. In addition, don't feel pressured into using *all* analytical tools; stick with a couple to begin with, work out which best meet your needs, and perhaps decide to expand on your selection a little bit further down the line.

If you have any recommendations for free social media ROI reporting tools that are not mentioned here, please contact me via the details at the end of the book and I'll look to get them added as soon as possible!

# How to Measure Facebook ROI Metrics: EdgeRank and Insights

**Explaining EdgeRank**

You cannot start to talk about measuring the marketing impact and potential ROI of the content you post on your Facebook Page without first talking about EdgeRank. EdgeRank is a Facebook-designed algorithm that determines what posts will appear on people's News Feeds, whether it be from their friends or Pages. Consider this: when you log into Facebook, you don't see *all* of the updates from *everyone* you're friends with or Pages you have liked in your News Feed. If this was the case, you would be absolutely swamped! Facebook did once try a "no filtering" experiment in 2009, and users didn't like it one bit. EdgeRank exists to filter stories to show those that it believes you are most relevant to you and your audience.

EdgeRank has three important variables:

**Affinity:** this is how much affinity a person has for your brand. In short, if they've liked or commented on your post at sometime in the past, you're more likely to show up in their News Feed now and in the future. Affinity only works one way, however; no matter how much you comment on their activity, it has no direct impact on how often they'll see you.

**Weight:** Facebook sees everything you publish as an "object." Each interaction (comment or like) an object gets adds to its weight, increasing the chances it will appear in someone's News Feed. That makes it easier for said people to comment on it, helping it to show on even more News Feeds and increasing the chances of additional comments and likes.

**Time:** no matter how popular your update may be, over time it's no longer "news" and it's chances of showing up in a News Feed decreases. Research suggests that the "lifetime" of a Facebook post is around 7 hours, and that most engagement occurs within 30 minutes of it being published.

For brands, the harsh reality is that when people like a Facebook Page, the majority never voluntarily return to it ever again. Instead, they rely on Page posts appearing in their News Feeds to keep them updated. In order to give your content the best chance of appearing in as many of your fans' feeds as possible, you need to get them *engaged* with your content.

There are plenty of tactics you can use to make your Facebook content as engaging as possible, but this book about return on investment isn't the best place for it. For tons more detail and advice, check out my bestseller, *500 Social Media Marketing Tips.* For now, here are a few key bullet points to get you started:

- Use photos and videos
- Ask questions
- Keep updates short
- Post regularly and consistently
- Post when your target audience is online
- Drive traffic from other social networks and your blog
- Experiment with Facebook advertising
- Don't automate your posts

**Facebook Insights**

Facebook Insights is an analytics tool for Facebook Page administrators that allows you to track the progress of Pages over time. However, it isn't just about the Likes and Unlikes your page receives - that's just one ROI metric you can gather (and as you know, not really the most useful one at that) - it's also invaluable in showing you how individual types of posts are performing.

Regularly monitoring the metrics available on Facebook Insights will help you to assess the size and impact of engagement from the content and discussions made on your Page. You can choose the duration period you want to view the metrics, and from analyzing the data, you can decide which content works best, who you are reaching, and where you can improve.

As I have discussed,  knowing the make-up of your target audience is very important, and Facebook Insights can also offer essential information to help you to improve engagement, and better understand the core audience that your page attracts.

Facebook Insights can be accessed from the top of your Facebook Page, and its default landing tab is the Overview, which will show you the following metrics:

**Total Likes -** The number of unique people who have "liked" your page.

**Friends Of Fans -** The number of unique people who were friends with fans who liked your page.

**People Talking About This -** The number of unique people who have created a story about your Page. A Story is created when someone likes your Page; posts to your Page Wall; likes, comments on or shares one of your Page posts; answers a question you posted; responds to an event; mentions your Page; tags your Page in a photo; checks in at your Place; or recommends your Place.

**Weekly Total Reach –** The number of unique people who have seen any content associated with your Page during the past 7 days. This includes Ads and Sponsored stories pointing to your Page.

Below this information is a chart of your activity, and a list of all of your posts with the following metrics for each:

**Reach -** The number of unique people who have seen your post in the first 28 days after it was published

**Engaged Users -** The number of unique people who have clicked on your post in the first 28 days after it was published.

**Talking About This -** The number of unique people who have created a story from your Page post in the first 28 days after it was published. Stories are created when someone likes, comments on or shares your post; answers a question you posted; or responds to an event.

**Virality -** The percentage of people who have created a story from your Page post out of the total number of unique people who have seen it.

**Other Facebook Insights Tabs**

The 'Likes', 'Reach' and 'Talking About This' tabs will provide you with a more detailed breakdown of the information gathered in the Overview tab, with data about the demographics and locations of the people your Page's content is reaching.

**Note:** Click the 'All Post Types' drop-down menu to select a particular sort of post (image, question, etc.) and click the name of each metric to toggle its numbers from highest to lowest.

**Exporting and Analyzing Facebook Insights**

At the top of the Facebook Insights page is an 'Export Data' button. Click this and Facebook will allow you to export your data directly to Microsoft Excel (.xls) or comma-separated text format (.csv). You can choose from Page level or Post level data, and a Data range, with a maximum of 500 posts at a time.

I recommend exporting this data at least once a month so that you are able to track your progress over time and align it with your overall social media strategy. If your content isn't working for you the way you expected, switch things up and experiment! Then, a month or two further down the line, check your Facebook Insights reports once again to see if things have changed for the better. If yes, fantastic! If not, see again what isn't working and try something new.

# How to Measure Pinterest, Instagram, and Tumblr ROI Metrics: The Reachli Suite

**Reachli**

Reachli (http://www.reachli.com) - formerly known as Pinerly - is a suite of tools designed to help content creators and sellers of goods easily post and measure the impact of their visual content onto social media sites, including Pinterest, Instagram, and Tumblr. Being a user since the days it was Pinerly, my main preference is to use it for tracking of Pinterest activity. Users can track the number of likes and re-pins a Pin receives (as on Pinterest), but more crucially, tell you how many times your Pin was clicked on through to your website or blog, and its overall reach.

With Reachli, you can create a Pin to be posted on Pinterest just like you would on the official site - by entering a URL, uploading from your PC, or grabbing an image from any site using the Pinerly bookmarklet. After entering a destination link and description, there is also a nifty image editing tool that allows you to tweak your image too - crop, resize, add text, brighten, etc.

Once live on Pinterest, Reachli provides a simple analytics tool to show you how your campaigns are being engaged with over time, allowing you to easily identify which ones are performing best. with this information at hand, you will be able to see if you need to make any changes to your efforts in order to increase their effectiveness.

# How to Measure Twitter ROI Metrics

### bitly

Bit.ly (http://bit.ly) is more than just a URL-shortening tool; it is one of the most popular and useful tools to help marketers track the success of the links they post on Twitter. It allows you to see the number of clicks, shares and saves your Twitter links have acquired over time, which webites were the top referrers, and from which countries your visitors were from.

### Twitter Counter

Twitter Counter (http://www.twittercounter.com) is brilliant website for analyzing your follower growth. Not only can you see a graph of your follower numbers over time, but you can also see your net new follows per day, and how this is likely to grow in the future. Handily, when you register, you are able to check a box that will send you a weekly update of your stats via e-mail.

### Hashtracking

Hashtracking (http://www.hashtracking.com) provides hashtag tracking and analytics. Generate a report for any Twitter hashtag, get snapshots of your reach, track your campaigns, and calculate your influence. You can also listen in on topics that you aren't discussing to gauge what kind of conversations are already taking place, then jump in when you're ready.

### Topsy

Topsy (http://www.topsy.com) is a search engine that uses proprietary data-indexing technology to give real-time insight into online conversations, which are relevant based on the calculated social influence of the conversation.

In simpler terms, you can use Topsy to see who is talking about you and your brand online via Twitter and Google Plus and who is linking to your content.

Some of the topics that you can for on Topsy are:

- Your name
- Your company/brand name
- Your product name(s)

- Your competition
- Your industry
- Your website URL(s) (leave off the “www”)
- Your email address
- Your employees’ names

Use Topsy to get an idea about what people are saying about you online, and use it as a way to plan and shape future social media marketing efforts.

# How to Measure LinkedIn ROI Metrics

If you're a Company Page administrator on LinkedIn, you can access Follower and Page Insights (metrics) from the Status Update module or in the Edit dropdown menu on the Company Page. With this, you have the ability to track a number of useful metrics, including:

- Total Followers
- New Followers
- Number of company updates you've posted and the increase or decreases over time
- Total impressions, engagement and change over the previous period
- Average Impressions per Update and change over the previous period
- Update Engagement and change over the previous period

A little further down the page you'll find charts and graphs, including detailed metrics on:

- Company Update Engagement (including a forward/back button to see previous periods)
- Follower Demographics (with appropriate sub tabs by Seniority, Industry, Function, Region, Company Since, and Employee)
- Company Update Impressions (including a forward/back button to see previous periods)
- Recent Followers (with a link to see more)
- Members Following (total followers with a forward/back button to see previous periods)
- New Followers (again, with a forward/back button to see previous periods)

# How to Measure YouTube ROI Metrics

Login to your YouTube account and you'll see an Analytics button in the top-right corner of the screen (the tool is also available from a menu inside Video Manager).

Whereas previously most marketers would concentrate on video's view counts, this is no longer the case. Audience retention stats are the new Daddy of YouTube metrics because they can tell you how engaged an audience is with your content. Someone who contributes a view count could just have clicked on your video, watched for 5 seconds and left, which is not much use in working out how well your video is really performing and how you can tweak your content to help push towards your overall business objectives and measure ROI.

The YouTube Analytics reports on views, demographics, playback locations, and traffic sources are all pretty self explanatory. And while they can give you a basic overall picture of your progress, audience retention is that much more important.

Click on this metric and YouTube will display the average view duration of your videos over the last 30 days. This is defined as the estimated average minutes watched per view, which you are free to target by more specific dates or by individual video (just search for it in the 'Content' box.

The Engagement reports can offer further insight into how the structure of your videos is encouraging the amplification of your content, with subscriber numbers, likes and dislikes, favorites, sharing, and comments all prominent metrics. Once again, I would refer you to *500 Social Media Marketing Tips* for a variety of ways to boost these metrics and increase overall engagement.

# How to Measure ROI Metrics With Google Analytics

Google Analytics is a fantastic free tool to help track several social media marketing metrics, and only takes a few minutes to setup. Google Analytics can track the impact of social media traffic on your site, going beyond clicks, re-tweets and other vanity metrics. While the following steps focus on measuring traffic and website conversions, this process can easily be adjusted to help measure metrics such as brand awareness or social media mentions, new website visitors gained via social networks, and the total number of social media followers.

- **Google Analytics can help you understand the users' social networks and their physical location.**

To see where in the world your social media traffic is coming from, you need to set up an advanced segment in Google Analytics.

When you're logged into your Google Analytics account, navigate to Advanced Segments, +New Custom Segment, then add your social media traffic sources to the segment. The rows of the table should read like as follows from left to right: Include -> Source -> Containing -> facebook.com (or whichever social network you want to track).

Once that's set up, navigate to Audience –> Demographics –> Location, and you'll be met with a grid that displays all of the locations and visits for your social media traffic. You can use this information to decide what locations you should best target with future campaigns and promotions, and work on areas where you want to improve your reach.

**Mobile Users**

As mobile users increase ever-more, specifically for social media sites, it is useful to track their visits separately, and Google Analytics allows you to do this. With that advanced segment selected (e.g. m.facebook.com), simply click over to Standard Reporting –> Audience –> Mobile –> Overview, and you'll see a chart that allows you to analyze your mobile traffic and compare it against other segments you have created.

If you receive a significant amount of traffic from mobile devices, you'll want to make sure your content displays well on smaller screens. If your overall business goal is to drive more sales and your website looks terrible on mobile devices, you will know that optimizing your site for these visitors is imperative to better your social media ROI.

**Setting Up Measurable Social Media Goals in Google Analytics**

One popular Google Analytics metric for social media is to find out which website sends you the best traffic. The 'best' traffic is that which converts to whatever you want your customer to do, and is defined as 'goal completions' in Google Analytics.

To set up social media goal tracking within Google Analytics, sign in and start by navigating to the "Admin" section of your dashboard, choose your site, and then select the "Goals" tab. Click to add one of 5 goals. Within Google Analytics, enter the Goal Name and you'll have the opportunity to set up four different types of goals:

- URL Destination
- Visit Duration
- Pages/Visit
- Event

If your site uses a single, defined "Thank You" page that's displayed following a successful purchase, you'll want to select the "URL Destination" goal option. On the other hand, if your site utilizes an off-site shopping cart provider or if your checkout process is dynamically generated, choose the "Events" option instead. In the Goal URL box, enter the last portion of the web address that you want to measure as people visit it. For example, if it is a 'thank you' page for making a purchase, where the URL ends in /thanks-very-much, enter '/thanks-very-much' (without the inverted commas and www.yourdomainname.com) in this space. Finally, click Save.

Once your Google Analytics goals are up and running, you should start to notice data appearing within a day or two, reflecting the sales or other conversions on your website.

**Tracking And Analyzing Your Goals in Google Analytics**

With Advanced Segmenting setup, you're ready to find out exactly where your traffic and conversion comes from. To see, navigate to the Overview page found within the Conversions section of Google Analytics, where you will see a record of all completed goal events that have occurred on your site.

The information here will initially include goal completions from all traffic sources, but click on the "Advanced Segments" button from within your dashboard in order to apply any of the Custom Segments you created earlier. Apply each of your Custom Segments to this data and make a note of the number of sales that have occurred as a result of social media participation across each of the different networks you're active with.

If you don't have a lot of referral sources, you can tell with a quick glance which social networks are working best for you without having to use advanced segments. However, if you have many referral sources, you might want to set up different advanced segments for each social network (e.g. facebook.com + m.facebook.com vs. t.co + twitter, for example for desktop vs mobile comparison).

Of course, not all traffic converts the first time they visit your site, so if you head to Standard Reporting –> Conversions –> Multi-Channel Funnels –> Top Conversion Paths, you will be able to see which social media sites are helping some of your other channels.

**How Google Analytics Can Help With ROI**

By measuring the traffic and goals completed via social media using Google Analytics, you will easily be able to tell which social media sites are working best for you, or where you need to improve. For example, if you are putting a lot of time and effort into Pinterest marketing but seeing minimal results, but notice that Facebook (a site where you are focusing a lot less) is converting much more successfully, you know either to adjust your Pinterest strategy or switch your concentration to Facebook.

www.ingramcontent.com/pod-product-compliance
Lightning Source LLC
LaVergne TN
LVHW040939150826
845672LV00008B/2441